WHAT IS A CAT?

Ron Hirschi

Photographs by
Linda Quartman Younker

Walker and Company
New York

For Lisa and all true cat lovers   R. H.
For Margaret in Aberdeen, generous care giver to all   L. Q. Y.

First published in the United States of America in 1991
by Walker Publishing Company, Inc.; first paperback edition published in 1998.

Published simultaneously in Canada by Thomas Allen & Son
Canada, Limited, Markham, Ontario

Library of Congress Cataloging-in-Publication Data
Hirschi, Ron.
What is a cat? / Ron Hirschi; photographs by Linda Quartman Younker.
p.   cm.
Summary: Text and photographs depict basic characteristics of the cat.
ISBN 0-8027-8122-5 (trade). —ISBN 0-8027-8123-3 (rein)
1. Cats—Juvenile literature.   [1. Cats.]   I. Younker, Linda
Quartman, ill.   II. Title.
SF445.7.H57   1991
636.8—dc20   91-13094
CIP
AC
ISBN 0-8027-7548-9 (paper)

Printed in Hong Kong
2   4   6   8   10   9   7   5   3   1

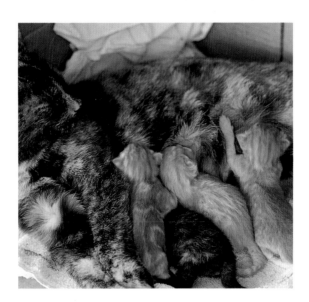

Cats are kittens . . .

kittens that pounce at the twitch
of a tail,

and run to drink morning's first
milk.

Cats are black as midnight,

orange as pumpkins,

and gray as clouds that bring the
rain.

All cats are curious
about birds and fish.

Cats stretch in the sun,

curl on your lap

and in your arms

and nap as only cats nap when
supper is done.

Cats jump,

up where they think we never
could reach.

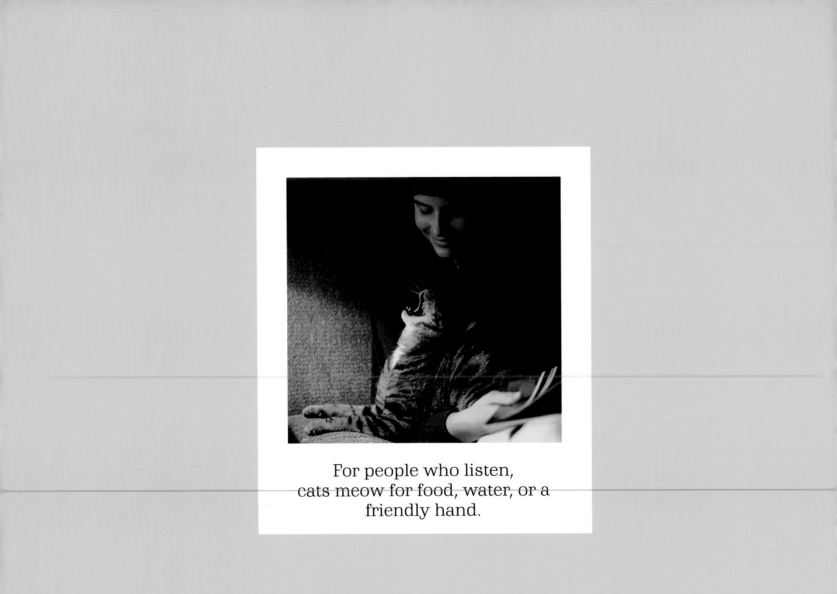

For people who listen,
cats meow for food, water, or a
friendly hand.

Cats purr to say
I love you.

Like most cat lovers, you probably talk to your cat. You might know that, in their own way, cats also speak to you. A meow says your cat is hungry or needs to go outside. A purr tells you when your cat is happy. Your cat will often be in the mood to play with you, but when it is tired, your cat will sneak off to a safe place and curl up for a nap.

To keep your cat healthy, feed it a balanced diet and have clean water available. Cats are meat eaters by nature, but well-balanced, nearly vegetarian diets (some milk and dairy products added) have been developed for cat owners who do not want their cats to eat so much meat. Talk with your veterinarian about food for your cat, and make sure its other health needs are taken care of.

To keep your cat from eating wild birds, keep it indoors during daylight hours as much as possible. To keep your cat from being a part of the sad overpopulation problem, have it spayed or neutered before it is old enough to give birth to unwanted kittens.